CHAIN BREAKER
(How to Break the Chain of Mental Health)

Gladys Macdonald

Copyright © 2024 by Gladys Macdonald.

ISBN: 9798890905017 (sc)
ISBN: 9798890905024 (e)

All rights reserved. No part of this book may be reproduced or transmitted in any form or by any means, electronic or mechanical, including photocopying, recording, or by any information storage and retrieval system, without permission in writing from the copyright owner.

The views expressed in this work are solely those of the author and do not necessarily reflect the views of the publisher, and the publisher hereby disclaims any responsibility for them.

EXPRESSO
Executive Center 777, Dunsmuir Street Vancouver, BC V71K4
1-888-721-0662 ext 101
info@expressopublishing.com

I would like to introduce myself; my name is **Gladys Macdonald** from **Georgetown, Prince Edward Island**. I am dealing with mental issues such as anxiety, panic attacks, depression, and, most importantly, suicidal thoughts.

CONTENTS

Introduction vii
From Childhood to Teenage Storms 1
My First Love 3
My First Marriage. 5
Battling Loneliness and Addiction. .7
Confronting Mental Health, Addiction,
and the Power of Positivity 8
Unwrapping the Holidays 10
Silent Struggles of Bullying 11
Harassment. 13
Wanted to have Children 17
Coping With Life 18
Struggle with Weight Loss. 20
Wanting people to Visit Seniors. .21
Trying to walk away from this Illness 22
We all Wear Masks 23
Emotional Stress 24
A Safe Place. 26
A Dark Nightmare 28
Fighting Our Demons when it comes to Mental Health 30
Living with O.C.D.. 31

Life Recovery 33
Believe you can and you are halfway there. 34
Let Go and Let God 35
Melissa's Story. 36
This is the Story of Kathy 39
Jane's Story 43
Emma's Story 47

INTRODUCTION

This Story is about mental health, and we deal with it every day, Such as anxiety, depression, panic attacks, fear and suicide also withdrawal from people, friends, and family sometimes loneliness. It can be caused from early child days growing up being abused in your marriages physically and emotionally also scared you for the rest of your life. So, if you are going through this, we can break this chain and live better, we know how day by day. If you need help call Mental Health at **1+(902) 838-0906** they are there to help always people.

FROM CHILDHOOD TO TEENAGE STORMS

I faced numerous challenges during my childhood, including a brain injury that led to fluid on the brain causing seizures and even a stroke on my left side, leaving my left hand disabled. However, that was just the beginning.

On May 21, 1961, a Sunday afternoon, I walked across the street to the store. As I was walking, I dropped pennies in a mud puddle. While picking them up, I found myself facing a pulp truck hauling wood as it backed out of the parking lot. The driver didn't see me, and I didn't see him.

The truck backed over me, with the two back wheels underneath me. Someone yelled at him to stay in the truck before the front wheel ran over me.

I suffered two fractured legs, and back then, they laid me on someone's front door as there were no gurneys available. I spent six months in the hospital, and at the age of six, my confusion, fear, anxiety flared up, and the rest followed.

As the teenage years approached, it became the worst time of my life, with other teenagers making fun of the way I walked and saying things that would upset me. Sometimes, I felt like I was a nobody I stayed in my bedroom after school and did not talk to my parents about what happened in school. I felt anxiety building and my heart was beating stronger like it was ready to pop out of my chest.

My Grandfather was bed riding, and one day my mom asked me to go upstairs to dump his potty because he could not get to the bathroom himself when I went to, bend down to pick his potty up his lend over and fondle me, I couldn't understand what he was doing to me. Then I told my mom she was mad and went upstairs to confront him today I am still living with that, it haunts me.

Also, in my teenage years. I was 13 years old and at that age, I started to be rebellious I never listened to my parents and I refused to come home when they told me to be home at a certain time. They would not let me do or go anywhere.

It was like having no life at all, they even had my young brothers following me up the street to see where I was going and report back to Mom and Dad, they were smothering me big time, and it made me trapped on edge. Then I started to get around friends and started to drink that the was only way I could cope with anxiety and other emotions but I did not stop I continued drinking. I ended up at Bars clubs and sometimes I didn't know where I was blanked out.

MY FIRST LOVE

I was 19 years old back then. I started going with this guy he was my first love; he was a gentleman and he treated me well. He was invited to my 16th birthday. A lot of girls were there and having fun with each other. I love him and he loved me.

Then he thought it was time to ask my parents if he could go steady with me, then my mother said

"Yes" - mom

My father said, *"no"* because he hated him and, it broke my heart, but we continued to sneak around unknown to my father. One day my love told me he was leaving Georgetown and moving to Toronto Ontario, he told me he still loves me and I always will, he told me that I was lost in the moment lonely empty, and for a moment.

I wanted to do something awful so I couldn't forget him, but it was too late he was already off to Toronto. I never heard from them again. Until the year 1997 when a friend came up to visit me, and told me to sit down, she said I have something to tell you before somebody else told you. Then she told me the names, that my first love had committed suicide she told me he hung himself.

I fell to the floor and I cried my eyes out. After my friend left, I locked my door and never answered the door or the phone for three days.

You see my first love was molested by a man who also did it to another guy and they took their own lives. How they suffer all their year with that and the bad memories of it by going through it and many others.

The people who are going through it today that is the reason why we have to break the chain of mental health but mind you it will get better as time goes on. I would like to talk about my two abusive marriages and how they affected me. One was Physical and the other was emotional abuse.

MY FIRST MARRIAGE

In 1985, I had my first marriage, and I was happy to be married to a nice man. Everything was going great, but after a year, things started to change. I was still drinking at that time, and he began to act strangely, which made me scared and uneasy.

I didn't know what to expect from him. He loved to hunt rabbits, and he had a lot of ammunition and guns in his safe, which made me anxious, thinking he might someday shoot someone, like me. The thought of it was always on my mind.

I wanted to get into his safe and get rid of his guns, but he had a bolt lock on it that nobody could open. As his mood changed, I found myself drinking more and more to cope with my fear.

Things continued to deteriorate, and one day, he threw a plate at me in a fit of rage. It missed me but almost hit me in the face. As the months passed, he treated me like a punching bag, mocking me in front of his friends and belittling me for not being able to cook like his mother. I would often retreat to the bedroom to cry; I hated him so much. This led to anxiety, fear, depression, and more.

We lived in a grand new home in the wilderness, and he isolated me from my friends and family as a way to assert control. He continued to abuse me emotionally and physically, and I felt powerless to stand up for myself.

I remember one day he came home from work, and when I asked about his day, he choked me. I told my family, but they didn't believe me. It felt like a nightmare I couldn't wake up from it.

Christmas was usually a joyful time for me, but that year, it was tainted by his cruelty. When I opened his gift, I found a rabbit trap set to close on my hand. He laughed at my distress, and I began to shake with fear and anger.

Eventually, he cut the phone line to prevent me from reaching out for help. He was cheating on me and eventually left me stranded. When I finally managed to contact my family, they came to pick me up.

In 1990, I filed for divorce, and I never saw him again. It was the best decision I ever made. I could finally breathe freely without constantly looking over my shoulder.

BATTLING LONELINESS AND ADDICTION

My next marriage wasn't much to talk about. I had quit drinking and was attending A.A. meetings, but my husband was a heavy drinker. When our monthly check came, instead of paying bills, he spent it all on liquor.

This brought back my anxiety and emotional abuse, with him calling me names and throwing things at me to hurt my feelings.

However, this time I had the upper hand. He was living in my mobile home, so I kicked him out. We were only married for three years, and I'm glad I made the right choice. I never remarried.

As the years went on, loneliness set in, especially during the fall and winter months. I felt empty and didn't want to go anywhere. I would panic at the sight of snow falling, knowing that ice would follow.

I want to talk about my alcohol problem. It wasn't good; I was a heavy drinker and a drunk. I felt guilty for putting my family through this, but alcohol was the only way I knew to ease the loneliness.

My attitude was awful; I cursed and swore at my parents and upsets my siblings. On February 18, 1989, I made a decision to quit.

CONFRONTING MENTAL HEALTH, ADDICTION, AND THE POWER OF POSITIVITY

I don't know if this is related to mental health but I hope it helps people who are going through this it will not take the pain away it will just make it worse. Turn your life around from drinking you'd be glad you did.

I had someone very special in my life and, she passed away from cirrhosis of the liver my mom was *56 years old*. Mental Health is not to be fooled with, it can leave you paralyzed and numb, not knowing where to turn we feel alone and helpless also scared we will have our depression flare up and more can happen, do you know that negative people can upset you also they can put you down, belittle you and make you feel like a nothing, it happens to me.

Then your health problem started up again. Positive people will never put you down they will lift your spirits and never take you for granted.

So, please stick with positive people it's really good for us going through mental health.

People who are taking hard drugs. Young older and also homeless people who live on the street with nowhere to sleep betting people money for food, trying to stay warm or cold winter nights even sharing needles to make them feel better.

This is also a part of Mental Health and wanting to get help by hoping for a better life and also to have people to talk with. For they can be lonesome.

I go to Mental Health meetings and like talk about how our week was, sometimes it is great, but sometimes it is awful because there is always something that upsets me. Then as we start talking about our problems things seem to be better. But when I have to go home. I start feeling lonesome and very down on myself. It is because I know I am going home to an empty house and, I know my emotions are going to start up again.

When I get like that, I do my deep breathing and it helps calm down. Meditation is a good method to help you. If you are going through a difficult time this can help a lot. Sometimes I think I would be out on the streets myself. If I had not stopped drinking my family would not put up with it. I would be on the street and it would be my fault.

UNWRAPPING THE HOLIDAYS

Christmas is a joyful holiday for many, but it can be a sad time for those living on the streets. They shouldn't have to spend Christmas alone on a cold night; they deserve care and love. It's crucial to break this cycle before it worsens and mental health deteriorates.

Personally, I love the holidays, like many others, but I often feel overwhelmed when they come to an end. Taking down the tree and decorations triggers emotions in me, and I find myself trying hard not to cry. I'm not sure what causes this reaction; perhaps something from my past triggered it.

Whatever the reason, it seems to stay with me. Maybe I feel this way because I fear it might be my last Christmas, and the thought of that upsets me. I hope to be around for a long time yet because I have many good things to do on this earth, like helping people with mental health through my book if it can make a difference.

SILENT STRUGGLES OF BULLYING

Bullying is due to mental health, especially in Teenagers in school and workplaces. Etc. it is hard to know when being bullied but there are signs, we can look for silence and not tell anyone what they are going through bullying is a form of aggressive behavior in which someone entirely and repeatedly does it.

Can cause another person or kids injury or discomfort. Bullying can take the form of physical contact, words, or subtle actions. Cyberbullying is a form of harassment on computers in which they can take their lives like overdosing on pills or doing harm to themselves.

I know I tried to do it myself like looking at my wrist it is still not easy for me today. So, I make a decision either I stay up on that mountain and get help or stay down off that mountain and not get help your decision, Mental Health meetings can help you. I stay up on that high mountain that is my decision. Mind you I'm still not well yet and probably will not be. I am trying every day but for me, it can be hard and challenging.

For me to get through this year, I can't believe the sickness, and accidents, I when through as a child. But now today I am going through a different kind of sickness it is called mental health and it has destroyed my life. Physical and emotional how I got that way like stress, panic, and anxiety, it will trigger seizures, it has been a long road for me.

But I have to work through it and never let go. Somedays I sat at home and tried not to think what if, I just ended my life so that there would be no more pain. Then something pulled me back that my life could be fixed if I continued to help myself to get better. To be with the people who are going through the same things as me.

I know my family loves me but I still feel that there is something in my life that I have lost over the years that brought on there, Physical and emotional side effects of anxiety, Panic attacks, etc. Life has not been easy for me but I hope someday it will get better.

HARASSMENT

Harassment is not to be fool with, a couple of years ago this guy lived in the same town as me. We also went together for those two years it was fine he started taking me out to dinner and I went at dinner. He started to act different like he'd look at girls' privates at the restaurant *"Oh!"*

"I like to have that in my bed "and people would hear him and it was embarrassing to me and I hated being with him. He was so ignored. One night he came in my house I ask him to come in big mistake.

He wanted to have his way with me and he did that when on for a while till, I call it off. Then the harassment started he start calling me. And saying he wanted to do me. I said no leave me alone. He kept calling and saying things that wasn't very nice.

I won't reply to his calls. Then one day he pulls in the driveway and came to my door I seen him coming and I ran in the bedroom for a couple of months he kept it up and my fear was getting really bad, and he wasn't about to stop.

He kept coming to my door the last of it I had to lock the door case he'd walk in for I was looking for trouble because I'd forget to lock it. Then the calls started up again and the knocks on the door. There were so many times running to the bedroom because of him.

I even had to look over my shoulder every time I went outside to check the mail or walk down street to the store. But one day he was behind me as I was walking down the street. He put the window down and was saying things that wasn't very nice, dirty words.

So, I had enough called the (R.C.M.P) Road Canadian Mountain Police. I wanted a restraining order against him, the police came down and told him he was not allowed to come near me.

It was all right for about three months then he started up again when you put a restraining order on someone it supposed to last six months.

But not for him, He was sending voicemails and also calling! It was never ending with. I call the RCMP again this time they call him to tell, He would be charging the next time.

He gets scare and never bother me until now not often. But enough to make me have fear all over again. Now he leaves messages and I just ignore him; I don't reply to him it only happens about once a month. But he still lives in the same town as me. Just up the street no to far from me.

Harassment is not healthy for people who are going through today's anxiety and a lot more. At night when the evening gets dark my window faces the roads there's a car that comes around and it drives slowly and I know it is him.

He was so obsessed with me that I was afraid for my life if you are with an obsessed person such as a man. Trust me they can make your life a living hell and women too. Obsessing can turn your mental health in a bad way and we don't need that.

Withdrawn from Social activities that aren't for me. I can't be a part of it. I choose not to, for me, it can cause stress shame, vulnerability, potential rejection, and more, underlying mental conditions. When I get to an A.A (Alcoholics Anonymous) meeting or any kind.

I'd walk in the room and just sit down; I don't mingle with anyone if someone comes over to me and says hello "How are you doing tonight?" I just said "GREAT, and you? "That's all that comes out of me.

I also withdraw when I drink. I have headaches, slow esteem, very sick, sweating, disoriented, and weak.

I even withdrew from my parents mostly my mother you see she would use the yardstick on us. And it hurt every time she broke me over us, she'd bring out another one, and I'd try to not be too withdrawn from her and those yardsticks but it was hard, my health condition was getting the best of me, My anxiety and fear.

I was afraid that tomorrow it would continue all over again. You could see it in my father's eyes how he saw how we were getting bet by Mom. If he tries to stop her, she'd say they have to learn to behave, so she out of it she'd tell him.

When I can't socially with people. I'd isolate myself; I don't know why. maybe because when I grew up, I had a lot of friends back then, that I could socialize with.

But today it would be different now. I don't have those anymore it is a different group of people today and it's really hard to socialize with these people, I don't have anything in common with them.

Maybe someday I will mingle with people but right now it's hard to socialize it will take time as for yardsticks, my mom bet over us. I shake when I see one today "How I would like to walk like others since my accident, at six years ago when a Pulp truck ran over me.

They couldn't straighten my left foot as it turned outward, they tried everything to straighten but they had no success.

"Oh!" How I wanted to be like other people.

It would upset me that they could walk normally I was so Jealous of them even today, I look at certain people and wish that for myself, Even run, skip, and jump I would cry knowing I could not do these things.

I even got made fun of. I get so depressed and alone sometimes and think to myself no guy wouldn't want to be seen with me the way I walk; I still think that today also my left hand is crippled due to a stroke. It's been a long road for me.

I will be 69 going on 70 next year and still wish could walk normally but loneliness is an issue.

Wanting to have that special in your life it might sound foolish but the loneliness in my life needs excitement.

"That was inside my mind right now"

Fulfillment even if it was a conversation with a gentleman, someone who won't take advantage of me, I'm sure a lot of us wanted through this. It's been a long time since my first love Ronnie, was in my life and I miss that.

But I still feel it will be a while before that will happen because of my disability. I know it sounds like I'm pulling myself down, But I know it is not right to feel that way right now.

I don't trust myself not only to fall in love again or believe in myself that things will get better but it will also help my Mental Health get stronger and help myself get through this day by day. That is what I want right now, also walk normally like other people.

WANTED TO HAVE CHILDREN

How I always wanted to have my own children. But my life had a different twist for me. I was told I couldn't have children because when I got hit by that truck, I was mangles inside I was devastated thinking that something like that could happen to me. It's torn me apart, I wanted to end my life.

But today it is getting better. I was to babysit for other people children and also my sister two boys, and it was a joy to be doing what I love. And it helps me to get over my problem by not having children and these children today have their own children.

Some women have mis caring and it must be really hard on them when I used to go to the store down street there be children walk in if they see me, they would run down and give me a big hug and it a blessing to have those big hugs.

I think I would have been a great mother, but unfortunately it wasn't in the cards. Today looking at a child smile whether it be on T.V or pictures of my own great, great grand nieces and nephews my brother from out west send me the smiles on their faces.

People I've meet always asked me if I have children of my own and I tell them "(Oh, I have)" everybody else children and that's alright with me. It's like having my own children.

COPING WITH LIFE

After my second divorce, I tried getting my life back on track. I really thought that being away from the mental and physical abuse, moving back to Georgetown closer to my family would be give me a more positive outlook on life, but it was far from the truth.

The years of negativity and belittling had shattered my self-esteem; I had no confidence in myself. I found it very hard to interact with people even with family members.

In my mind, I felt like a failure, that I wasn't good enough and didn't belong. I felt so sorry for myself, it was pathetic.

In 1997 my depression hit its peak. I had locked myself in my mobile home with the phone off the hook for days. On the fourth day I was finally able to think clearly enough to seek help.

I made an appointment to see a doctor after explaining the best I could as to what was going on his diagnosis was, we call it today "clinical depression" I should've been made to see a psychotherapist.

But instead, he suggested an anti-depression called Luvox. I have to say it did help for a while eventually I started to experience suicidal thoughts. The doctor then put me on Prozac, it did help with the suicidal thoughts, but it also made me tired and sleepy.

I wanted to stop taking the Prozac because of my tiredness also my bouts with depression were less frequent and less severe so I thought I could try coping on my own.

But he recommended against it and he was right. I realize now that I would have been right back where I started if I had.

I still have off days, times when I just want to be by myself. But it doesn't last very long. My confidence has improved and I think more positive thoughts then what I did before. Life still a way of bringing you down if you submit to it, So I am still working every day to think of all the good things in my life. Positive thinking can be hard at times but it sure beats the alternative.

STRUGGLE WITH WEIGHT LOSS

How I wish to be skinny again weight was always on issues for me and it started to bothered me until my young days, and my abuse marriages.

Food was my comfort and my friend but it also brought on depression and emotional failure known that I was fat and I was made him off and, it hurt me as well.

The more I gain it was very hard to loss everything. I'd try, I turned back to food, I had no willpower too stop it was like someone or something was calling out my name to eat food. It was embarrassing going places and have people stare at me.

When I was a teenager, I could even skirts, bathing suit and pretty tops. But no more now. I am any tops and pants. I also wear a brace on my leg that I have to wear every day, I'm still trying to loss my weight but I am still struggle but that's alright. Some people like and some don't, But that's "ok".

"Women and Men, if you are struggling with your weight don't give up keep trying you'll get there."

Bulimia and anorexia people know it hard for you, but have to get better you need nourishment, calcium and Protein to help you.

So, there's people who love you, your family and friends you have to do it for yourself if you want to get well. Hope I help you in a lot of ways. Mental Health meeting can help people also.

WANTING PEOPLE TO VISIT SENIORS

Living alone can be lonesome, especially for a senior citizen. There are signs we go through, like constantly looking out the windows and seeing the same thing day in and day out.

Silence prevails at times, with no ringing phones or door knocking. It's interesting to observe how mental health affects seniors; they may experience loneliness and other challenges.

As a senior going through this myself, sometimes the only companionship I have is the TV and my cat named "Bella." Unfortunately, I don't see my family often. When I ask them to bring me something from the store, their visits are brief.

I understand they work hard, but it would be nice if they stayed and talked for a while. Seniors depend on their families because, in the end, everyone will need help someday.

Looking into the eyes of a senior citizen reveals the sadness, anxiety, and more that they go through, especially those in a manor who have no family left to visit them.

There is a family that visits their mom every day—two daughters, a son, and his wife. Even on weekends, the feeling of being wanted is upsettingly rare for many, including myself.

This chain of neglect and loneliness needs to be broken. Let's come together and break this chain until we are free from the grasp of mental health.

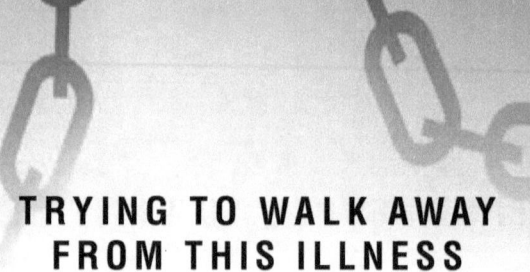

TRYING TO WALK AWAY FROM THIS ILLNESS

Dealing with illness is undeniably tough, and sometimes, it's hard to know if others truly understand what you're going through. Some days are manageable, but others can be extremely challenging, especially when your illness interferes with daily life.

I struggle with something called aura, which precedes my seizures and also affects my memory gradually. The medications I'm on are potent, and my doctor suggests increasing them further, which adds to the difficulty, especially considering its impact on my mental health.

As if that weren't enough, the harassment I mentioned earlier persists. The person continues to call and leave messages, triggering panic and causing me to lock the door.

This situation isn't healthy for us and exacerbates our illnesses. So, what can we do about it? We can't let it consume us. Mental health issues are daunting, but ignoring them isn't an option.

We need support from mental health professionals and others facing similar challenges. It's frightening, but together, we can navigate through it and offer each other much-needed support.

WE ALL WEAR MASKS

As we journey through life, we all wear masks. These masks are evident every day on people's faces, including my own. Sometimes they reflect anger, other times they showcase smiles, and occasionally they betray fear, loneliness, and more.

However, despite observing the external appearances of others, we rarely glimpse their true selves. This is particularly true for those grappling with mental health challenges.

We all experience them. Someday, when you encounter someone smiling on the street, you might sense that something isn't quite right; they don't want others to know what they're going through.

So, they wear a smile to conceal their pain. There are people in pain seeking assistance, such as those battling cancer. You can see it in their faces; they may never fully recover.

When encountering someone with cancer or any other illness, they often withdraw from others due to their condition, leading to anxiety, panic, and emotional distress. This is just one aspect of the suffering we endure every day while wearing our masks.

People may perceive me as angry and cranky, but that's not the truth. It's just that I've been through a lot due to my own problems and illnesses growing up. When people ask me if I'm cranky, I reply, "No, I'm fine." But deep down, I'm not fine.

Perhaps one day, sharing this will help others going through similar struggles. Our masks will always be a part of us.

EMOTIONAL STRESS

Emotional stress is a significant part of my life. It can ruin the way I live. There is anxiety, loneliness, and depression, along with crying when I am alone, thinking about past events that upset me.

Just as other people who go through emotional stress, I too desire to get well, knowing we have a long way to go.

However, we will get there if we all work together. Emotional stress can cause a lot of pain, such as heart issues and losing people who are no longer around.

Moreover, going into debt and owing money to people or companies which I cannot pay, and dealing with thoughts of suicide every day. It's been a long road for me, and I don't think it will get any better for a while to come.

But I can work on it by thinking happy thoughts and maintaining a positive outlook as I walk through this world.

So, I advise those who are going through mental health issues to work on their emotional stress by practicing deep breathing and engaging their five senses. Five things you see, four things you can hear, three things you can touch, two things you can smell, and the number one thing you can taste — that is an exercise.

You can do it, and it can also help with meditation. All of these things are really helpful for emotional stress and for people with other troubles. So, I hope you get a little help from me *"You know Why?"* by helping yourself; it's also helping me.

A SAFE PLACE

We all have a safe place that we can go. My safe place is my home, a place where the birds sing and the river flows. It is like meditation for me when I have emotional stress and am going through really bad days with upsetting thoughts that scare me. This is when my mental health really suffers.

If you are going through this, go to your safe place wherever that may be, and meditate or just sit and listen to all the sounds around you. It's good for you, that's why I love spring; it gives me peace of mind, as it will for you.

There are days when I just like to stay home, knowing that I am safe and nobody can hurt me; it is also my safe haven. Mental health is one of the worst things we go through, affecting our dignity and the way we look at things in our lives.

As we look in the mirror and see our reflection, we are trying to find ourselves and help ourselves and other people with what they are going through by finding their safe place too.

For me, sometimes my safe place doesn't help me on very disturbing days. Just curling up in my chair and forgetting this world ever existed.

When friends and family bring up past mistakes, it upsets me; it makes me cry and anxious, and it can even lead to the worst thing of all: Which is suicide.

That's why I don't want my family and friends to make decisions for me. I can decide for myself; I wish people would leave me alone in my safe place.

Pressuring me is not going to help my mental health. If you are going through this, you are not alone.

A DARK NIGHTMARE

Before my first marriage in my 20s, as I was just developing into a woman and didn't know what making love was all about, it was a new thing for me. But I was about to find out. There was a bar I went to; it was a wonderful place, and I happened to be there with a friend.

I got to know a lot of people there, even a couple of guys a little older than me. We talked a lot, but I didn't know them well enough. As the night went on, my friend was ready to go home; she asked me if I was coming with her, and I said later.

A couple of minutes passed, she asked me again, and still, I said, "No."

The two guys who were there said they would take me home when my friend left. I stayed for a little while longer, then the guys were ready to take me home. As they were driving, they turned onto a different road, and I asked them,

"Where are we going?" They said, "*We will go home in a minute; would you like to come in?*" So, I did.

They asked me if I wanted a drink, and I said water.

When I drink the water after a minute, *I feel dizzy*, I guess they put something on that water I drink.

After that, I don't remember a thing; all I know is when I woke up, one of them was on top of me, and the other one was standing, looking on us.

I didn't want to tell this story because nobody would believe me, or it did not happen, but it was a complete nightmare.

Today, it still haunts me; one of the guys died, and the other is still alive. I hope I never meet him again.

FIGHTING OUR DEMONS WHEN IT COMES TO MENTAL HEALTH

We all face challenges in our lives such as suffering, hatred, jealousy, and revenge. Additionally, we grapple with our inner demons when it comes to mental health. We try to evade them, but it's difficult, knowing that we require ample assistance to overcome them.

However, we can support each other. Not only can we confront these demons, but we can also conquer them so they no longer haunt those of us afflicted by this illness. With faith and healing, we can defeat these demons; these are the essential elements we need. Without them, we have nothing.

I encourage you to address any issues that trouble you and engage in activities that keep these demons at bay, so we can recover and cultivate the positive mindset we need today. I'm not sure if my message resonates with everyone, but I hope it provides some assistance.

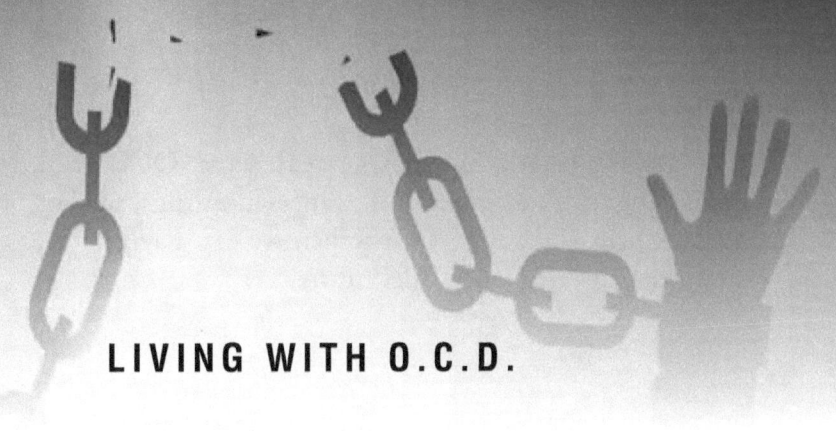

LIVING WITH O.C.D.

Obsessive-compulsive disorder (OCD) is a mental health condition characterized by persistent and uncontrollable thoughts (obsessions) and repetitive behaviors (compulsions). These symptoms can be time-consuming and cause significant distress, interfering with daily life.

OCD often leads to feelings of fear, anxiety, and more. There is currently no cure for OCD, and it can persist in the background, even when it no longer actively disrupts one's life. I struggle with OCD daily.

I find it difficult to control my obsessions and compulsions, which can involve unwanted thoughts, images, or impulses that trigger intense emotions.

Additionally, I am also a hoarder, a common manifestation of OCD where I have difficulty discarding items. Despite my efforts to seek help, I understand that OCD does not have a definitive cure.

However, with the support of others, we can work towards managing and alleviating the symptoms of OCD.

Living with OCD is challenging, as there is no guaranteed way to rid oneself of it. Nevertheless, we hold onto hope for advancements in treatment and ultimately, a cure.

It's important for those experiencing OCD, as well as those struggling with addiction to substances like drugs, alcohol, or gambling, to seek help and support. Together, we can navigate these challenges and work towards a healthier future.

LIFE RECOVERY

Life in recovery with mental health challenges can be difficult to navigate. It can alter our lifestyles and hinder our progress in terms of how we feel and behave as we strive to overcome these obstacles, such as anxiety and fears.

In my own journey, I'm endeavoring to recover, but it proves challenging, particularly in finding a path forward. I've undergone various stages of recovery, yet achieving full mental health may be a prolonged process. Regardless of the time it takes, I commit to making progress every day.

Recovery entails reclaiming what we've lost or had taken from us, as well as restoring our health from illness. All of us must heed the signals our bodies send us; otherwise, true recovery may elude us.

In my personal experience of recovery, I've faced challenges stemming from past events, such as my first two marriages and a childhood accident.

However, I've struggled to form new relationships due to lingering fears and mistrust, often choosing partners who aren't right for me. Overcoming this fear is a priority for me, though it may take time.

Ultimately, my health is paramount, which is why I'm dedicated to living a life focused on recovery and wellness. I encourage others to embark on their recovery journeys, as it's a path toward a healthier and happier life.

BELIEVE YOU CAN AND YOU ARE HALFWAY THERE

As children, we tend to believe that things will get better as we grow up. But as we age, we begin to ponder the true meaning of life.

There are happy times and there are bad times, but regardless of what we face, we will overcome. People grappling with mental health issues often yearn for a miracle to alleviate their suffering. Someday, that miracle may come, and we can bid farewell to this illness.

I've been battling this for as long as I can remember, and anyone else going through this will also find their way. All we need to do is believe, and the rest will fall into place.

As we journey through life, we come to understand that change is inevitable.

We see ourselves striving for wellness, embracing life as it unfolds, being true to ourselves, and, most importantly, loving ourselves—it's crucial for our mental health and much more.

Therefore, believe you can, and you're halfway there - embrace life to the fullest, have patience, and hold onto hope, faith, and love. With these three pillars in our lives, we can believe in the presence of hope.

LET GO AND LET GOD

Have you ever experienced one of those days where you can't seem to lay your head down because you have so much on your mind? It's like navigating through the worries of life, including depression, anxiety, and other mental health challenges.

In those moments, it feels like there's always someone watching over us. For many, that someone is God, a constant presence by our side every day. He has helped me through my stroke and many other challenges.

He's there for me, and He's there for you too if you allow Him. Finding comfort in His presence can help us navigate through any situation.

When we witness others suffering, we often see ourselves in their struggles, and we recognize the need for divine assistance.

Dealing with mental health issues may take time, but having faith in God's guidance is crucial. There's a saying: "Ask and you shall receive, seek and you shall find, knock and the door shall be opened unto you." It emphasizes the power of reaching out to God for help and guidance.

Your story about letting go and letting God is powerful and meaningful. Even if it may seem confusing at times, trusting in a higher power can lead to healing and prosperity for many. So, I encourage you to let God help you. That's why this story is called "LET GO AND LET GOD."

MELISSA'S STORY

We have a long road of healing and a long road to walk before things get better what we will get there. As we walk that road it will get easy, and easy. It will take some time however but we are trying to work at it. I've been walking this road for a long time trying to get better but I'm not heal.

I'm still walking that road but will get to the end of it someday. As will you, A lot of people get depression and upset that things will never get better believe me, I think the same way but we have to have faith. Sometimes I really have great days and other days I'm suffering.

I can't focus on anything and sometimes I just sit and cry and feel sorry for myself but, I'm trying to get well for it is going to be a long road for me also. Oh! If I can find a way out of this sickness of Mental Health I would even if it was for one week for a freedom to walk the road of healing.

I would surely to be it. You can walk that road of healing to take a change it might be a long road but it will be a healing road someday.

My life is somewhat, Yet, from time to time, I'm waiting for the other shoe to drop- bracing. I come from a family where abuse was "normal". It was usually my older brother who was brain damaged at birth that viciously beat me of tea.

Regardless, I was always told it "Wasn't his fault he can't help it. Nobody bothered to tell 0–18-year-old me that I should have been protected- at least my parents, much later. I was informed that the reason none of the kids would play with me or my sister was because of our older brother.

Later, we were avoided because of our younger brother also.

It's been said that our personality is developed from childhood experiences. If that is so, I must be pretty messed up. *"Hahaha"*

I've been chased by a mad older brother with a butcher knife many, many times. I've been thrown down the stairs several times resulting it stitches to the head.

I've been driven into the corner of an old solid wood TV cabinet. I got several inner and outer stitches out of that one. This was in the 1970's. Incredibly, no medical personnel or literally anyone reported it.

Somewhere along the line years age. I lost or suppressed many memories. In the last several years, the memories began to come back. Some are partial, and some are horrific. My brother's actions in particular were totally disturbing and distressing. The details about the incidents are so upsetting that I rarely speak of them.

One incident memory that recently, in the past few years, is that of the time when the neighbor friends and I actually, I just witnessed it", Emptied my uncle's liquor bottle onto the ground. We stuck around to watch the reaction. *"Bad idea"* He saw us, grabbed my dad is shotgun, and chased us up the back field.

Thankfully, my friend and I found cover in thick brush. I've never been so scared in my whole life. My uncle was bad shit crazy enough to fire the shotgun, but we had all scattered and hid.

Even to present time, I still have trouble assessing potentially violent situations. Because substance abuse was prevalent in my family. The men I got involved were almost all addicted to alcohol or drugs. I got treated really badly from them all because I thought it was normal and I was worthless.

I still, to this day have to rethink and deem myself worth for healthy relationships.

I feel guilty that oldest child is addicted to alcohol. His wife and children have already experienced alcoholic tirades. I pray that he will have the courage to get his drinking under control.

It seems that the curse of addiction has skipped a generation. I feel so helpless in trying to get him help. I fear that something really bad has to happen "wake him up", and get him to stop.

THIS IS THE STORY OF KATHY

In 1983, I met this guy at a dance, and we had a good time dancing almost every dance. After the dance, we went to a party and enjoyed ourselves. He drove me home afterward, and I wasn't sure if I would see him again.

Then, one day at work, I ran into him, and we talked for a bit. He then asked me if I wanted to go out that night, and I said yes. We started dating, and eventually, he asked me to marry him, to which I also said yes.

Things went pretty well for the first couple of years, but living with his parents and his aunt, things started going wrong as they began interfering in our marriage. If we had a disagreement, they would take his side, and after about a year of it, I had enough and left, going to stay with my parents.

I stayed there for about a month, and Joe decided to move out there with me. Things seemed to be going okay, but it wasn't perfect. I suggested that maybe we should get our own place, so we did.

Again, things seemed to be on the right track for a while, but about six months of living on our own, Joe decided that we couldn't afford it, so we moved back to his parents. That was a big mistake as things just got worse. So, in 1989, we separated, and I moved to Charlottetown and got a job as a banquet waitress. I loved it, but I got involved with the wrong group of people and ended up losing that job, and moving back in with my parents.

In 1990, I got divorced and was single for about three years. I met this guy, and he seemed like a great guy. We didn't date very long before we decided to get married. We lived with my parents for a while until they offered to help us with rent on the place where I grew up.

Things were going great for the first couple of years, then Henry started drinking again, and things suddenly went downhill. One day, I was getting my hair done, and Henry came in, saying he wanted to go to town to grocery shop, so I said, "OK." When I was done getting my hair done, and we were getting ready to leave, he said, "You drive," and I asked, "Why?" He replied that he was drinking and didn't want to drive. So, I said I wasn't going shopping if he was drinking.

He persuaded me to go, which was a very big mistake because when we finished shopping, he wanted to go look for a friend but couldn't find him. So, he wanted to go to a bar to search for him.

He went in and came back asking for money to pay to get in. I said "no," as I wanted to go home, and we got into a big fight. He grabbed my purse to get money, but I grabbed it and ended up ripping the handle off.

So, I said **OKAY**, I would give him the money to get in. He came out a while later and wanted me to go in, but I said "no," so he got out and came to the driver's side, attempting to haul me out, but I grabbed the steering wheel.

Eventually, he reached in and took the keys out of the ignition before returning inside. I waited for a while and remembered he had a hidden spare key. I found it, left and went home.

Around 3 am, the phone rang, and it was Henry telling me to get into the van and come get him up the road, so I did. He was furious and told me to "get over it" as he drove back to the house. When we got home, I was going up the steps when he came up behind me and shoved me. As I was trying to unlock the door, he kicked me.

When I got the door open, he shoved me so hard I landed in the living room where he continued to kick me. When he stopped, I got up and went back to bed. Henry came in and wanted to have sex but I said no but he wouldn't stop and forced himself on me.

I told him in the morning when I was going to work, I wanted him to be gone when I got home that wasn't going to live like that. When I got home from work, he was waiting for me and wanted to talk to me so I said OK.

He apologized for what he did and promised me that he would never do anything like that again. I told him that if he ever did, I would divorce him.

Things were going well, and my dad mentioned that someone was interested in buying the house, but we didn't have the resources to stay. So, we had to find a new place to live. We found a reasonably priced apartment that also had a building the landlord said Henry could use for his bodywork and mechanic work.

We lived there for a couple of years, but then some friends offered us a big house with an extra bedroom, so we moved there, and Henry set up his body shop.

However, the landlord eventually decided to sell the house, so once again, we had to find a new place to live. Things were great after we bought a piece of land and moved the building we were living in onto the property.

We worked hard to expand the building into a house, doing all the work ourselves.

A short time after the abuse started again only verbal at first and usually when he was drinking.

One night he was drinking and I was trying to write a resume and he started touching me and wanted to have a sex but I kept asking him to stop till I finished what I was doing, but he kept it up till I got mad shouted at him to leave me alone, the next thing I knew I was airborne and landed on a ceramic pot on the floor missing the picture window by inches.

He tried to help me up but I told him to get away I didn't want his help.

I then decided to go to bed and he came in and of course want s*x. So, I get up and went out to lay on the couch. He followed me and started removing my clothes; I couldn't stop him. He then went to bed and got up a few hrs later to go to work.

My back was hurting so I looked at it in the mirror and had a bruise the size of a grapefruit. About a week later I was getting undressed and he noticed it and asked how I got it I told him but he never apologized for it.

Things never got any better do eventually I left with my stuff to my parents and stayed in their camper for the summer. Dad fixed up a place for me to live. I filed for divorce in 2008 and went to abuse counseling for a year and was so glad I did.

JANE'S STORY

For as far back as I can remember, I was an anxious child. I worried about everything, had separation anxiety, and got upset at the slightest things. I didn't find comfort in my parents. One of my earliest memories was me sitting on the floor, sobbing uncontrollably while my mother stood laughing and snapping a picture.

Once, my father forgot to pick me up from preschool, and the teacher had gone home. I stood on the sidewalk, frozen in fear, convinced I had been abandoned. I would rather have died than gone to a house for help; I was nonverbal to anyone outside my family.

This became a family joke many years later, but for me, that feeling of dread still washed over me as if it were yesterday. I got separated from my mother at the grocery store once and ended up upstairs in the manager's office, so distraught I couldn't even speak my name. And there was the time when the babysitter lost me on the beach, and some strangers handed me over to the police.

So, it seemed my confidence in those around me was diminished before I reached elementary school, and my level of anxiety and stress had escalated far beyond what I thought was typical for a five-year-old.

My primary years were awkward; I had few to no friends. We moved countries twice, changing schools, and I spoke differently. It's very hard to be the new kid. I didn't fit in, I didn't have the right clothes, my hair was curly and wild. School was both stressful and boring.

I didn't want to be there; I wanted to be home, in my own safe space, with my animals.

My father used to say, "Wipe that look off your face." I didn't know what he was talking about and always felt like that was an unfair statement. I had earned the reputation in the family of being bossy, sooky, easily triggered.

I have very few childhood memories, if any, of being truly happy. I started to hide bread in my room. I found comfort in eating it alone, and that, at age eight, was the start of a lifelong struggle with food and how it made me feel.

By grade six, I was trying so hard to fit in, but it was impossible. I fought with the boys and exchanged the dreaded cold shoulder with the girls. At age twelve, I overdosed with an entire bottle of over-the-counter pain relief.

I spent the night in the hospital being treated, and it was never discussed. Not once did I have the conversation of what, where, and when with either of my parents. I felt that I had embarrassed them.

Junior high started to look a bit better as I changed schools and met "the wrong crowd" who accepted me. We'd hang out at the smoking doors or skip out and cram into someone's car and get wasted. The years of drug experimentation had begun.

My mother died when I was fifteen. My father consoled himself with a whiskey bottle, and my older brothers had already moved out. I quit high school and terminated a teen pregnancy that year. I was angry and very lost.

I grew up too fast and ended up in unhealthy relationships with substance and emotional abuse. The partying carried on until my early twenties when something made me come to my senses, and I got my GED. This led to college and finally a diploma.

My career spanned 24 years, and life was in turmoil. I had become money-driven, very motivated, but a workaholic and miserable. I was intense, a micromanager, and angry. I would be yelling one minute and crying the next. I was up and down and all over the place. I was diagnosed as having Bipolar II disorder.

I tried antidepressants at first but didn't like them, didn't really give them a chance. I tried therapy, thought it was ridiculous. The therapist told me to discover my inner child, and I excused myself. I wasn't having any of it.

Fast forward through twenty-five years, I had changed employers more than ten times, gone back to college twice, moved houses exactly twenty times. My behavior was erratic, I was terrible with money, had grandiose plans and ideas, my mind was full of rapid thoughts, and my speech was pressured. I felt like a ticking time bomb. I was so angry and demonstrated fits of rage at partners, employers, whoever disgruntled me or hurt my feelings that day. I am not proud of my behavior during this period; I have a lot of regrets.

I married and divorced, moved across the country in the hopes that the grass was greener. It wasn't. The same work, life, partner, money troubles followed me, as did my behavior and inability to manage stress.

The night shift and circumstances at work contributed to a year-long severe depression that overcame me. I felt like I couldn't keep my head above water; I was drowning in quicksand. I would sit feeling paralyzed, literally not being able to move.

I wasn't functioning. Very dark thoughts entered my mind, and I experienced suicidal ideation daily. I had a plan and had access to the materials necessary to carry it out. Somehow, I managed to drive myself to the emergency room. It was Christmas Day.

I stayed in the psychiatric unit for 31 days, discharged with a proven diagnosis of Bipolar II with Rapid Cycling. I took the meds, I went to groups, I saw my psychiatrist, I did everything they told me to do. I was very fortunate to be able to leave work for an extended period to take care of myself properly.

Today my life consists of keeping it simple, surrounding myself with people who understand and support me, recognizing when my mood is shifting and acting accordingly.

I have hobbies that make me happy and volunteer opportunities that are rewarding. I am living proof that things can get better and that a Bipolar diagnosis doesn't mean you can't lead a fulfilling life.

EMMA'S STORY

As the author of this narrative, I am not just a storyteller but an advocate for mental health, seeking to weave words that resonate with the hearts of those who have weathered the turbulent seas of their own minds. With an understanding born from personal experiences and a profound empathy for the struggles that accompany mental health challenges, I embark on this storytelling journey with the intention of offering solace and understanding.

"In sharing this story, my hope is to contribute to the ongoing dialogue surrounding mental health, breaking down stigma, and fostering a supportive community for those who have felt the weight of their own minds. This is not just a story; it is an offering of understanding, a virtual hand extended to those who may find solace in knowing that they are not alone in their journey toward healing and resilience."

Once upon a time in the small town of Sunflower village, lived a young woman named Emma. On the surface, Emma appeared to be leading a perfect life. She had a loving family, supportive friends, and a promising career.

However, beneath the facade of normalcy, Emma struggled silently with her mental health. Emma had been grappling with anxiety for years, but it wasn't until recently that her anxiety attacks escalated into full-blown panic attacks.

The triggers were unpredictable - sometimes it was the pressure at work, other times it was the overwhelming expectations she placed on herself, and occasionally, it was the crowded places that sent her spiraling.

One day, as Emma was navigating through her demanding job, the mounting stress reached a breaking point. She felt a tightness in her chest, her palms became sweaty, and an overwhelming sense of dread washed over her. Gasping for breath, she rushed to the restroom, desperate to escape the prying eyes of her colleagues.

Alone in the bathroom, Emma sank to the floor, her heart pounding in her ears. She felt trapped, as if the walls were closing in on her. Tears streamed down her face as she grappled with the irrational fear that something terrible was about to happen.

As the panic attack subsided, Emma knew she couldn't keep battling this internal storm alone. She decided to confide in her best friend, Sarah, who had noticed Emma's struggles but wasn't aware of the severity.

Over a cup of tea in Sarah's cozy living room, Emma hesitantly shared her experiences with anxiety and panic attacks. Sarah listened attentively, providing a comforting presence that Emma desperately needed. With Sarah's encouragement, Emma decided to seek professional help.

One day, the mounting stress reached a breaking point as Emma navigated through her demanding job. Overwhelmed, she rushed to the restroom, where a panic attack consumed her. Feeling trapped, she decided it was time to confide in her best friend, Sarah, who had noticed Emma's struggles but wasn't aware of their severity.

Over tea in Sarah's cozy living room, Emma shared her experiences with anxiety and panic attacks. With Sarah's encouragement, Emma decided to seek professional help. Therapy sessions became a transformative journey, equipping Emma with coping mechanisms and strategies to navigate anxiety's waves.

Emma's decision to open up extended to her family, who unexpectedly offered support and understanding. Gradually regaining control over her mental health, Emma embraced mindfulness, exercise, and self-care.

Her journey transformed her into a mental health advocate in Sunflower Village, where she established a support group for those facing similar challenges.

Yet, as Emma became more open about her struggles, not everyone responded with empathy. The small town witnessed judgment and misconceptions, and Emma faced bullying for her vulnerability.

Refusing to be defined by others' opinions, Emma found strength in her vulnerability, confronting the stigma surrounding mental health.

She shared her story publicly, not just about overcoming anxiety but also about facing the stigma and bullying. Emma's courage inspired others, leading her to give talks at local events and schools, challenging preconceived notions about mental health.

Her advocacy transformed Sunflower's perception of mental health, with her support group becoming a haven for many.

Emma's resilience became a symbol of triumph, challenging the town's mindset. The same people who doubted her strength witnessed her transformation into a powerful advocate.

As Sunflower Village embraced a more compassionate mindset, Emma's journey became a lesson that true strength lies in supporting each other through life's unseen battles. The town learned that by embracing vulnerability, they could collectively foster a more inclusive and empathetic community, forever changing the narrative around mental health in community.

Emma began attending therapy sessions, where she learned coping mechanisms and strategies to navigate the waves of anxiety. She also opened up to her family about her struggles, finding unexpected support and understanding.

Though the journey was challenging, Emma gradually regained control over her mental health. She embraced mindfulness techniques, engaged in regular exercise, and prioritized self-care. The support of her loved ones, coupled with professional guidance, helped Emma emerge stronger than ever.

Through her experience, Emma became an advocate for mental health awareness in the Village. She started a support group for those facing similar challenges, creating a safe space for sharing stories and fostering a sense of community.

In the end, Emma's story was not just about overcoming anxiety and panic attacks; it was about breaking the stigma surrounding mental health and finding strength in vulnerability. The small town of Sunflower Village learned an important lesson - that sometimes, the strongest battles are the ones fought beneath the surface.

Dedication

I want to take a moment to express my heartfelt gratitude to everyone who has believed in me and supported my journey. Your encouragement has been invaluable, and I am deeply grateful.

I thank my friends and family for always believing in my vision. Your faith in me has given me the strength to keep going.

To the mental health community, I am honored to be a part of such a compassionate and understanding group. Your shared experiences and openness have been a source of inspiration and strength. I hope my book will provide solace and support to those navigating their mental health journeys.

To the individuals who generously shared their stories for this book, thank you. Your courage and honesty have made this book possible, and I am deeply grateful for your contributions. Your stories will undoubtedly resonate with and help many readers.

My book is a testament to the power of shared experiences and the importance of mental health awareness. It is my sincere hope that it will offer comfort, understanding, and hope to all who read it.

Also, I would like to thank my agent Lucas Flores for everything.

Let's break the chain together!

www.ingramcontent.com/pod-product-compliance
Lightning Source LLC
LaVergne TN
LVHW041553070526
838199LV00046B/1948